VEGE COOKING CARIBBEAN STYLE

Ayesha Williams

LMH Publishing Limited

First Edition
10 9 8 7 6 5 4 3 2 1

Cover Design by: Eunice Pereira/Leequee & Riley
Edited by: Kevin Sean Harris
Book Design, layout & typesetting by: Eunice Pereira/Leequee & Riley

Published by: LMH Publishing Limited
7 Norman Road,
LOJ Industrial Complex
Building 10
Kingston C.S.O., Jamaica
Tel.: 876-938-0005; 938-0712
Fax: 876-759-8752
Email: lmhbookpublishing@cwjamaica.com
Website: www.lmhpublishingjamaica.com

Printed in Jamaica
by : XPRESS LITHO LTD

ISBN: 976-8202-17-3

Acknowledgements

Without the encouragement of my friends and family, this book would have remained in my head on the table. For encouraging me to share my recipes with the world, I would like to thank my sisters, Jewel and Carey-Anne Williams, my mummy and all my aunts, for my first introduction to the discipline of cooking, and Terence for always asking me "so when's the book coming out?"

Thank you Dad, Gunther, Charles, Ianir, Marco, Andrew, Betty, Lleana and all my friends in Puerto Rico and the Dominican Republic. Thank you Eunice for the beautiful layout and design, and Enrique and Orlando for the last batch.

There are of course all my other friends who having tasted my creations, asked me to write a few recipes down. To all of you, thank you for your support…now you can buy the book.

Quick Tip

A quick way to get great vegetable stock is to add 1 pack of vegetable soup mix to 6 cups of water and bring to a boil. Allow this mixture to simmer over a low flame for 10 minutes and let cool. This mixture can be used as a base for all your soups and sauces.

Traditional Vegetable Stock
4 carrots, large, sliced
2 cups celery, chopped
3 onions, chopped
1/2 cup butter
2 teaspoons thyme leaves, minced
2 bay leaves
Salt and pepper to taste

Ready!
In a large soup pot over medium heat, melt butter and sauté carrots, onions, celery, thyme leaves and bay leaves for 10 minutes. Add 8 cups of water and bring to a boil. Let simmer over low flame for 2 hours. Using a cheese cloth for strainer, remove all vegetable, season with salt and pepper and use remaining stock as a base in your favorite soups and sauces.

SOUPS

"IRIE" PEPPER-POT SOUP

A Cool Blend Of Callaloo And Greens

Dumplings

1 1/2 cups all-purpose flour
1 teaspoon salt
Water

Ready!

In a small bowl, combine flour and salt. Add enough water to form a soft dry ball. Divide the ball into 14 parts. Roll parts into little balls. Dust with flour and set aside.

Soup

4 1/2 cups vegetable stock
1 cup onions, roughly chopped
1 1/2 cups carrots, roughly chopped
1 cup escallion, roughly chopped
2 cups callaloo, fresh, roughly chopped (spinach)
2 cups callaloo, boiled (pureed)
1/4 cup coconut milk
2 tablespoons crushed pimento (all spice)
1 whole scotch bonnet pepper
1/4 cup butter

Ready!

In large soup pot, heat butter and sauté onions, carrots and escallions for 1 minute. Stir in 2 tablespoons flour then add vegetable stock. Mix well. Let mixture boil for 3 minutes on high flame. Reduce flame and add crushed pimento and whole scotch bonnet pepper. Add dumplings and chopped callaloo. Boil for 5 minutes over medium flame. Add puree of callaloo and coconut milk. Season soup with salt and pepper to taste. Let simmer over low flame for 10 minutes. Serve with lightly buttered garlic bread.

"WICKED" PUMPKIN SOUP

A Spicy Pumpkin Soup With A Touch Of Coconut Cream

Soup

3 1/2 cups vegetable stock
2 cups pumpkin, roughly chopped (peeled, seedless)
1 cup onion, roughly chopped
1 cup carrots, roughly chopped
1 cup escallion, roughly chopped
1 cup celery, roughly chopped
1/4 cup vegetable oil
2 teaspoons flour
1 cup coconut milk
Salt and pepper to taste

Ready!
In a large soup pot, heat vegetable oil and sauté onions, escallion, celery and carrots for 1 minute. Stir in 2 teaspoons flour. Add vegetable stock to vegetable. Add pumpkin and let boil for 12 minutes over medium flame. Pour contents of soup pot into blender, puree soup with vegetables for 2 minutes or until smooth. Pour puree back into soup pot and add coconut milk. Season with salt and pepper and let simmer for 5 minutes. Served with bread sticks.

Garnish

1/2 cup sweet potato strips
1 teaspoon cinnamon
1/4 cup vegetable oil

Ready!
In a small frying pan heat vegetable oil and fry sweet potato strips until crisp. Remove from frying pan and sprinkle strips with cinnamon. Place a small amount of fried sweet potato strips on top of each serving of soup.

Quick tip

Serve this soup with toasted bread strips slathered in garlic butter. This is a great accomplishment and will complement the smooth taste of this savory soup.

"BASHMENT" CALLALOO SOUP

A Nice Puree Of Callaloo, Coconut Milk And Vegetables With A Hint Of Roasted Garlic

Soup

3 cups vegetable stock
3 cups callaloo, chopped
1/4 cup onions, chopped
1 cup carrots, chopped
1/4 cup escallion, chopped
6 cloves garlic roasted
3/4 cup coconut milk
Salt and pepper to taste

Ready!
In large soup pot bring vegetable stock to a boil. Add callaloo, onions, carrots and escallion. Let boil over medium flame for 10 minutes. Pour soup into blender and add roasted garlic. Puree for 2 minutes or until smooth. Return soup to pot and add coconut milk. Let simmer for 5 minutes and season with salt and pepper.

Garnish

1/2 cup bell pepper, red, julienne
1/2 cup bell pepper, yellow, julienne

Ready!
Place bell pepper julienne on a baking sheet. Roast in a 360° degree F oven for 10 minutes. Let cool. Remove from baking sheet and top each serving of soup with peppers.

"LAWD IT SWEET" LENTIL SOUP

A Filling Soup Of Lentils, Boiled Yams, Sweet Potatoes With A Touch Of Basil

Soup

2 cups lentils, dry, soaked in water over night
4 cups vegetable stock
2 cups yams, boiled, cubed
1/2 cup onions, sliced
3 cloves garlic, minced
1 cup carrots, sliced
1/2 cup escallion, minced
1 whole scotch bonnet pepper
Salt and pepper to taste

Ready!
Boil lentils in vegetable stock for 2 hours over low flame or until cooked (pressure cooker could be used to shorten time by 1 hour). Add onions, garlic, carrots, pimento (all spice) and escallion. Add whole pepper and let boil for 10 minutes over medium flame. Remove whole pepper. Add boiled yams and sweet potato cubes. Add basil and let simmer over low flame for 5 minutes. Add salt and pepper to taste.

Garnish

1 cup carrot strips
Salt and pepper to taste
1/4 cup vegetable oil

Ready!
In a small frying pan heat vegetable oil and fry carrot strips until crisp. Remove from frying pan and sprinkle strips with salt and pepper. Place a small amount of fried carrot strips on top of each serving of soup.

"JAMMIN'" RED PEAS SOUP

A Thick Soup Of Red Peas And Dumplings Spiced Up With Scotch Bonnet Peppers

Dumplings

1 1/2 cups all-purpose flour
1 teaspoon salt
salt

Ready!
In small bowl, combine flour and salt. Add enough water to form a soft dry ball. Divide the ball into 14 parts. Roll parts into little balls. Dust with flour and set aside.

Soup

1 1/2 cups dry red-peas (7oz., soaked in water over night)
4 cups vegetable stock
1 cup onion, julienne
1/2 cup carrots, diced
1/2 cup celery, diced
1/2 cup escallion, minced
1 whole scotch bonnet pepper
4 cloves garlic, minced
1 cup veggie chunks (TSP)
2 cups yam, boiled, cubed
1 cup sweet potato, boiled, cubed
Salt and pepper to taste

Ready!
In a large soup pot, cover red peas with vegetable stock and cook for 1 1/2 hours over low heat or for 1 hour in a pressure cooker. Add garlic, onion, pimento (all-spice) and celery. Add dumplings, sweet potato, yam and veggie chunks. Let soup boil for 10 minutes over high flame. Add carrots, salt and pepper to taste. Let simmer for 5 minutes and then serve.

"OCHO RIOS" POTATO SOUP

A Smooth Puree Of Irish Potatoes

Soup

3 cups potato, boiled, diced
3 cups vegetable stock
1/4 cup onions, chopped
2 tablespoons garlic, minced
2 tablespoons butter
2 tablespoons flour
1/4 parsley, chopped
1/2 cup coconut milk
2 basil leaves, fresh
1 whole scotch bonnet pepper
Salt and pepper to taste

Ready!

In soup pot sauté onion and garlic in butter. Mix in flour and vegetable stock. Bring vegetable stock to boil. Add potatoes, whole scotch bonnet peppers and basil. Let boil for 10 minutes, remove whole peppers from liquid. Puree soup in blender for 2 minutes or until smooth. Return soup to soup pot and add coconut milk. Stir over low heat. Season with salt and pepper and serve hot. Garnish with mint parsley.

Quick tip

When preparing a soup puree, make sure that all ingredients are properly cooked. This will help to ensure that the proper result is smooth and not grainy. There is nothing worse than a grainy puree so take care to ensure that your soup is smooth.

SALADS

FERN GULLY

Tropical garden salad sprayed with citrus vinaigrette. Page 17

TRELAWNY

Cucumber and tomato salad laced in a basil and garlic dressing. Page 19

GARDEN PARISH

Heart of palm salad topped with coconut salsa. Page 21

YALLAHS

Traditional garden salad garnished with golden yam bites and laced with a papaya dressing. Page 23

MOUNT ROSSER

Pasta tossed with onions, tomatoes and olive oil served atop a bed of romaine lettuce. Page 25

PUERTO SECO

A bound salad of potato and yam in a spicy pesto sauce on leafy greens. Page 27

FERN GULLY

Tropical Garden Salad Sprayed With Citrus Vinaigrette

Citrus Vinaigrette

3/4 cup orange juice
1 teaspoon lemon juice
1 teaspoon vinegar
2 teaspoons olive oil
1/4 teaspoon black pepper

Ready!
Whisk together orange juice, lemon juice, vinegar, olive oil and black pepper in large bowl. Set aside.

Salad

1 large head of romaine lettuce
1 cup iceberg lettuce, chopped
1 large orange, peeled, segmented
1/2 cup raisins
1/2 cup carrot, shredded
1/2 cup bell peppers, red, julienne
1/2 cup bell peppers, yellow, julienne

Ready!
Toss salad ingredients in bowl with citrus vinaigrette and arrange on plate as in picture.

Quick tip

When you arrange the salad on separate plates, pay attention to the evenness of colour. Ensure that the plate flows with an even balance and that it is not overcrowded with lettuce or other greens.

TRELAWNY

Cucumber And Tomato Salad Laced In A Basil And Garlic Dressing

Dressing

1/2 teaspoon salt
1/2 teaspoon pepper
1/2 cup olive oil
1 teaspoon basil
1/2 teaspoon garlic powder

Ready!
In large bowl whisk together salt, pepper, olive oil, basil and garlic powder. Set aside.

Salad

1 cucumber, large, halved and sliced
1 cucumber, small, peeled, diced
2 tomatoes, large, finely diced
1/2 cup black olives, diced
1/2 cup Gouda cheese, cubed
1 eggplant, large, thinly sliced
1/4 cup vinegar

Ready!
Cover sliced eggplants in vinegar and let sit for 3 minutes. Heat a heavy skillet for 3 minutes over high flame. Reduce flame and pat eggplant slices dry with a paper napkin. Place eggplants in the hot skillet for 1 minute or on each side. Remove from pan and set aside. Toss cucumber, tomato, olive, cheese and eggplant in dressing and follow picture for plant presentation.

Place eggplant slices in the middle of each plate. Using a sharp knife split the sliced cucumbers down the middle. Arrange as in picture around the eggplant. Fill the cavity with the remaining diced vegetables.

Garnish

Top with roasted bell pepper, Julienne (see "Bashment" Callaloo soup recipe on page 7).

GARDEN PARISH

Heart Of Palm Salad Topped With Coconut Salsa

Coconut Salsa

1 cup coconut, shredded
1 cup tomato, diced
1/2 onion, minced
2 teaspoons parsley, minced
1/2 cup coconut milk
Salt and pepper to taste

Ready!
Blend the coconut, tomato, onion, parsley and coconut milk for 10 seconds. Season with salt and pepper and set aside.

Salad

1 cup heart of palm, julienne
1/4 cup sweet pickles, sliced
1/4 cup pickles, julienne
1/4 cup bell peppers, red, roasted, julienne
1/4 cup bell peppers, yellow, roasted, julienne
1 head romaine lettuce

Ready!
Arrange vegetables on bed of romaine lettuce as in picture and top with coconut salsa.

Garnish with bread sticks.

YALLAHS

Traditional Garden Salad Garnished With Golden Yam Bites And Laced With A Papaya Dressing.

Papaya Dressing

1 papaya, peeled, deseeded
1/2 cup vinegar
1/4 cup onions, minced
2 cloves garlic

Ready!
In blender, puree papaya, vinegar, onion and garlic for 1 minute or until smooth.

Salad

1 head iceberg lettuce
1 large tomato, cut into wedges
1/2 carrots, julienne
1 cup yam, boiled, peeled
1 egg
1 cup bread crumbs
2 tablespoons cornmeal
1/2 cup vegetable oil

Ready!
In a small bowl whisk one egg. Add yam to egg mixture. Remove yam from mixture and cover with breadcrumbs and cornmeal. Heat vegetable oil in a small frying pan. Fry yams until golden brown. Remove from oil and let cool. In large bowl toss lettuce, tomato and carrots in papaya dressing. Arrange salad in plate and top with fried yams.

MOUNT ROSSER

Pasta With Onions, Tomatoes And Olive Oil Served Atop A Bed Of Crisp Romaine Lettuce.

Salad

2 cups tricolour butterfly pasta, cooked
1 cup tomatoes, minced
1/4 cup onions, minced
6 cloves garlic, minced
1/2 teaspoon pimento (all spice), crushed
1/4 cup olive oil
1 head romaine lettuce
3 teaspoons coconut milk powder
Salt and pepper to taste

Ready!

In large frying pan, heat olive oil and sauté onions and garlic for 1 minute. Reduce flame and add pasta, tomato and pimento (all spice). Add coconut milk powder, salt and pepper and mix well. Present this dish by mounting the pasta mixture on a bed of romaine lettuce as in the picture.

PUERTO SECO

A Bound Salad Of Potato And Yam In A Spicy Pesto Sauce On Leafy Greens

Pesto Sauce

1 cup basil, fresh, chopped
1/4 cup pine nuts
1 cup olive oil
2 cloves garlic

Ready!
Place basil, pine nuts, olive oil and garlic in blender or food processor and puree until smooth. Season with salt and pepper and set aside.

Salad

1 cup potatoes, boiled, cubed
1 cup yam, boiled, cubed
1 cup Gouda cheese, cubed
Salt and pepper to taste
1 head Iceberg lettuce
1 head Romaine lettuce

Ready!
In a medium bowl combine potato, yam, cheese, salt, pepper and pesto sauce. Place potato and pesto sauce. Place potatoes and pesto mixture atop a bed of Iceberg lettuce.

MAIN COURSES

SURPRISE INSIDE

Sour and sweet vegetables in crepes served aside fried green plantain chips. Page 31

BANANA BOAT

Vegetable quiche on a green banana crust garnished with deep fried carrot strips in a savory béchamel sauce. Page 33

CURRY NICE

Boiled dumplings filled with veggie mince in a rich curry sauce. Page 35

REAL JERK

Jerk soy steaks topped with a savory brown sauce, served aside vegetable risotto and stir-fried vegetables. Page 37

REGGAE PIZZA

Whole-wheat pizza crust with tomato sauce, vegetables, veggie mince and goat cheese. Page 39

STRICTLY DE BEST

Three layers of vegetables, cheese and veggie chunks topped with mozzarella and Parmesan cheese served atop prego tomato sauce. Page 41

VEGETABLE MOFUNGO

A wicked combination of green plantain and veggie chunks in a savory brown sauce. Page 43

ST. BESS

Canolis filled with veggie mince, covered in black bean sauce and served aside yam risotto. Page 45

SURPRISE INSIDE

Sour And Sweet Vegetable In Crêpes Served Aside Fried Green Plantain Chips

Crêpe

3 eggs
1 cup milk
Salt and pepper to taste
3/4 cup whole wheat flour
4 teaspoons margarine

Ready!
In a blender, blend milk, eggs, flour, salt and pepper until smooth. Allow mixture to sit for 1 hour at room temperature. Place a crêpe pan or a non-stick pan 7-8 inches wide over a low flame for 2 minutes. Coat bottom of pan with 1 tsp. margarine. Pour about 1/4 of the mixture into the pan. Let cook over low flame until the edges are firm or slightly coloured. Turn and brown on the other side. Repeat and set aside.

Plantain Chips

1 plantain, large, green, thinly sliced lengthwise
2 cups vegetable oil
Salt and pepper

Ready!
In a deep frying pan heat the vegetable oil. Dust plantain chips with salt and pepper. Place strips in the hot oil and cook for three minutes or until chips are cooked.

Sour and Sweet Vegetables

1 cup almonds, roughly chopped
1/2 cup mushrooms, cooked, sliced
1/2 cup broad beans, tin
1/2 cup carrots, julienne
1/2 cup onions, julienne
1/4 cup broccoli, minced
1/2 cup bell pepper, red, minced
2 tablespoons butter
1 teaspoon cornstarch
Salt and pepper to taste
1/2 cup honey
1/2 cup vinegar

Ready!
Place 2 tablespoons butter in saucepan, over medium heat. Sauté onion, carrot, bell pepper and mushrooms for 1 minute. Add chopped almonds and cornstarch. Mix well. Add broad beans and broccoli and lower the flame. Add 1/2 cup vinegar and 1/2 cup honey. Season the vegetables with salt and pepper to taste and let reduce over low flame. On serving plate, place vegetables in crêpe and serve. Garnish with plantain chips.

BANANA BOAT

Vegetable Quiche On A Green Banana Crust Garnished With Deep Fried Carrot Strips In A Savory Béchamel Sauce.

Banana crust

1 1/2 cups green banana, cooked
1/2 cup butter, melted

Ready!
In a food processor or using a fork, combine banana and butter until smooth. Spread banana mixture evenly out on the base of a 9" quiche pan. Set aside.

Savory béchamel sauce

3 tablespoons butter
1 1/2 tablespoons all purpose flour
1 tablespoon pimento (all spice)
Salt and white pepper to taste
1 onion, halved
2 3/4 cups whole milk
1 teaspoon oregano

In a medium heavy saucepan, melt butter over low heat. Mixing flour to form a roux. Continuing mixing in the flour and let cook until the mixture smells nutty (about 2-3 minutes over low flame). Turn off the heat below the flour mixture. In a small pan, heat milk to a soft boil, (this process is called scalding). Reheat the flour mixture over low flame and whisk in scalded milk avoiding lumps. Continue to incorporate all the ingredients with a whisk over a low flame. Add the onion, pimento and oregano. Allow mixture to cook over a low flame for 10-15 minutes. Mixture should appear thick and creamy. Using a cheese cloth chinois or fine-mesh strainer, remove all vegetable from the sauce and discard. Season with salt and pepper and set aside.

Quiche

1/2 cup broccoli, minced
1/2 cup mushrooms
1/2 cup onion, minced
3 cloves garlic, minced
3 tablespoons bell pepper, minced
2 tablespoons butter
4 eggs
1 cup gouda cheese, shredded
3/4 cup coconut milk
1 1/2 tablespoons all purpose flour

Ready!
In medium mixing bowl, whisk eggs adding salt and pepper. In frying pan sauté onion, garlic, mushrooms and bell peppers in butter over low flame. Add flour to cooked vegetables and combine. Add coconut milk to mixture and add veggie cheese. Remove the pan from the heat and slowly mix in the whisked eggs stirring constantly. Pour mixture into prepared crust and bake at 360° degrees F for 20 minutes. (Optional) serve atop creamy béchamel sauce.

Deep Fried Carrot Strips

1 cup carrot julienne
3 tablespoons vegetable oil

In a small frying pan, heat vegetable oil and sauté carrots for 3 minutes. Remove from oil and pat dry. Serve atop quiche.

CURRY NICE

Boiled Dumplings Filled With Veggie Mince In A Rich Curry Sauce

Dumplings

1 1/2 cups all purpose flour

Water

1 teaspoon salt

Ready!

In a small bowl combine flour and salt. Add enough water to form a soft dry ball. Divide the ball into 14 parts. Roll parts into flat squares. Dust with flour and set aside.

Filling

1 cup texturized vegetable protein (T.V.P. mince)

3 1/2 cups vegetable stock

1 teaspoon garlic, minced

1/2 cup onion, minced

1 tablespoon butter

Salt and pepper to taste

Ready!

In a small bowl soak T.V.P. mince in 1 cup water. In small frying pan sauté onion and garlic in butter and add T.V.P. mince. Add 1 1/4 cups vegetable stock and salt and pepper. Let reduce over high flame for 5-10 minutes. Drain T.V.P. mince and reserve the liquid. Spoon 2 teaspoons of mince onto the prepared dumpling dough and close dough to form a small rectangle. Repeat until the dough is finished. Pour reserved liquid into a medium sized pot. Heat liquid and add 1 1/2 cups vegetable stock. Bring contents of pot to boil and add dumplings. Let dumplings cook for 10 minutes over a high flame. Remove dumplings from stock and set aside.

Curry sauce

1 cup vegetable stock

2 tablespoons curry powder

1 teaspoon pimento, ground (all spice)

1 tablespoon butter

1 cup coconut milk

Salt and pepper to taste

Ready!

In medium saucepan, bring vegetable stock and pimento (all spice) to a boil. Add curry powder and coconut milk and let boil for 5 minutes over medium flame. Season sauce with salt and pepper and finish the sauce by adding the butter. (Thicken with a mixture of 1 1/2 teaspoons cornstarch and 2 teaspoons of water if needed). In serving bowls, cover dumplings with curry sauce and garnish with escallion or parsley.

REAL JERK

Jerk Soy Steaks Topped With Savory Brown Sauce, Served Aside Vegetable Risotto And Stir Fried Vegetables

Jerk Sauce/Marinade

1 cup dark sugar
1/4 cup cane vinegar
1 whole scotch bonnet pepper
2 tablespoons pick-a-pepper
1/2 cup dark rum
2 tablespoons pimento (all-spice)
1/4 cup ginger

Ready!
In a blender, process sugar, vinegar, whole scotch bonnet pepper, rum, pimento, ginger and pick-a-pepper sauce until smooth. Set aside.

Steaks

4 T.V.P. steaks/patties (tin, texturized vegetable protein)

In medium bowl, marinate T.V.P. steaks in jerk marinade for 10 minutes. Place steaks on a greased baking tin in a 360° degree F oven for 10 minutes uncovered. Remove and serve atop vegetable risotto.

Vegetable Risotto

1 cup carrots, minced
1 cup onion, minced
7 cloves garlic, minced
5 teaspoons butter
2 cups vegetable stock
1 cup Parmesan cheese powder
1/2 cup coconut milk
1 cup Arborio rice

Ready!
In a large frying pan, sauté onions, carrots, garlic and rice in 3 tablespoons butter and add 1 cup vegetable stock. Let cook for 5 minutes over a high flame and stir constantly. Add 2 tablespoons butter and 1/2 cup coconut milk and reduce the flame. Mix in 1 cup vegetable stock and add Parmesan cheese. Let reduce over low flame for 3 minutes. Remove from flame.

Stir Fried Vegetables

1/2 cup bell pepper, julienne, red
1/2 cup bell pepper, julienne, green
2 tablespoons butter
1/2 cup bell pepper, julienne, yellow
1/2 cup onion, julienne

Ready!
Heat butter in large frying pan and sauté bell peppers and onions. Season vegetables with salt and pepper and serve aside risotto and jerk soy steaks.

REGGAE PIZZA

Whole Wheat Pizza Crust Topped With Tomato Sauce, Vegetables, Veggie Mince And Goat Cheese

Pizza Dough

1 1/2 pkg. (2 tablespoons) active dry yeast
3 tablespoons vegetable oil
1 teaspoon sugar
1 teaspoon garlic salt
1 1/4 cups warm water
1 teaspoon oregano
1 cup whole wheat flour
2 cups all-purpose flour

Ready!

In a large bowl, mix in yeast with warm water. Add vegetable oil, garlic salt, sugar and oregano. Add all-purpose flour. Beat until smooth in electric mixer. Using a wooden spoon, mix in wheat flour until firm dough is formed. Remove dough from bowl and knead lightly on floured surface for 6 minutes. Dough should be smooth. Place dough in a greased bowl, cover and let rise in a warm place for 45 minutes. Spread dough onto a 10-12 inch pizza pan and bake for 10 minutes at 400° degrees F. Remove dough from oven and cover lightly with tomato sauce and set aside.

Pizza Toppings

1 cup veggie mince, cooked
1 cup bell peppers, julienne
1/4 cup onion, julienne
1 cup goat cheese, shredded
1/4 cup mushroom, halved
1/4 cup broccoli, minced
1/4 cup olives, black, whole

Ready!

Top the semi-cooked dough with toppings. Place pizza back in oven at 400° degrees F for 10 minutes. Remove from oven and serve hot.

Tomato Sauce

1 cup onion, minced
1/4 cup olive oil
1 cup of Prego tomato sauce
1/2 cup tomato paste
4 cloves garlic, minced
1 teaspoon oregano
1 teaspoon basil
Salt and pepper to taste

Ready!

In a saucepan, sauté onions and garlic in olive oil over a medium flame. Add tomato sauce, tomato paste, oregano and basil, and stir well. Season with salt and pepper and let reduce for 6 minutes over high flame.

STRICTLY DE BEST

3 Layers Of Vegetables, Cheese And Veggie Chunks Topped With Mozzarella And Parmesan Cheese Served Atop Prego Tomato Sauce

Lasagna

6 strips lasagna, cooked

Filling

2 cups veggie chunks, soaked in water, drained
1/2 cup onion, minced
1/2 cup carrot, minced
1/4 cup celery, minced
2 tablespoons basil, fresh, minced
2 tablespoons vegetable oil
Salt and pepper to taste
1 cup Prego tomato sauce
1/2 cup vegetable stock
1/2 cup Parmesan cheese
1 cup Mozzarella cheese, shredded
2 tablespoons parsley, minced

Ready!

In large saucepan, heat vegetable oil and sauté onion, carrot, celery and veggie mince. Add vegetable stock and season with salt and pepper. Add thyme and Prego tomato sauce and let reduce for 5 minutes over low flame. Grease a large rectangular baking tin with butter and line the bottom of the tin with 1 layer of lasagna. Cover the first layer of lasagna with veggie mince mixture and 2 tablespoons Mozzarella cheese and Parmesan cheese. Place another layer of lasagna to cover the veggie mince and repeat filling until you have 3 layers. Top with Mozzarella cheese and remaining parsley, and bake at 360° degrees F for 20 minutes. Serve atop Prego tomato sauce and garnish with parsley or celery.

VEGETABLE MOFUNGO

A Wicked Combination Of Green Plantain And Veggie Chunks In A Savory Brown Sauce

Mofungo

I cup veggie chunks, soaked in water, drained
1/2 cup onion, minced
1/4 cup escallion, minced
2 tablespoons basil, fresh, minced
2 teaspoons parsley, minced
2 tablespoons vegetable oil
3 cloves garlic, minced
1/2 cup vegetable stock
I teaspoon Jamaican hot sauce
2 tablespoons tomato paste
2 1/2 cups green plantain, boiled

Ready!
In large saucepan, heat vegetable oil and sauté onion, garlic, escallion and veggie chunks. Add vegetable stock and basil, and season with hot sauce, salt and pepper. Add tomato paste and mix well. Let cook over high flame for 2 minutes and stir constantly.

Brown Sauce

I tablespoon dark sugar
2 1/2 cups vegetable stock
1/2 cup tomato paste
I onion, roughly chopped
3 tablespoons Jamaican pick-a-pepper sauce
I tablespoon all-purpose flour
I carrot, roughly chopped
I tomato, roughly chopped
I tablespoon browning

Ready!
In large skillet, heat I tablespoon vegetable oil. Sauté carrots, tomatoes, onions, celery, and dark sugar over a high flame until the mixture caramelizes. Add 2 tablespoons flour and mix in the tomato paste. Carefully add vegetable stock and let reduce for 3 minutes over a medium flame. Add pick-a-pepper sauce and browning. Let reduce over high flame for 3 minutes. Use a metal sieve to strain the mixture removing all the vegetables. Discard vegetables and set aside.

Assembly of Mofungo!

In a large mortar, pound green plantains, veggie chunks mixture and parsley. Mixture should be rough in appearance and not smooth. Spoon the hot mixture into a 4 oz cup or mold to give the Mofungo some form. Carefully invert cup into plate, releasing the Mofungo onto the plate. Garnish with deep fried carrot strips, parsley and lace with savory brown sauce.

ST. BESS

Canolis Filled With Veggie Mince, Covered In Black Bean Sauce And Served Aside Yam Rissotto

Canoli

12 large canolis
1 tablespoon olive oil

Ready!

In large pot, bring 4 cups of water to a boil. Add olive oil and canolis. Cook for 5 minutes and drain. Set aside.

Filling

2 cups veggie mince, cooked
1 tablespoon parsley, minced
1/4 cup escallion, minced
3 cloves garlic, minced
Salt and pepper to taste
1/4 cup evaporated milk
1/2 cup celery, chopped
1 cup black bean sauce, tin
1/2 cup goat cheese, shredded

Ready!

In a blender, blend veggie mince, parsley, onion, escallion, garlic, celery and heavy cream. Season with salt and pepper and add goat cheese. Fill canolis with veggie mixture and place in a greased casserole dish. Top with black bean sauce and bake at 325° degrees F for 20 minutes. Serve with yam risotto.

Yam Risotto

2 lbs yellow yam, boiled
1 cup butter
1 1/2 cups evaporated milk
1/2 cup vegetable stock
1/4 cup Parmesan cheese powder
2 tablespoons olive oil
1/4 cup onion, minced
1/4 cup garlic, minced
1/4 cup escallion, minced

Ready!

Finely dice boiled yams. In large frying pan, heat olive oil and sauté onion, garlic, and escallion. Add yams and evaporated milk. Reduce flame and add vegetable stock, let simmer for 5 minutes. Add butter, salt and pepper to taste. Mix in parmesan cheese. Mixture should appear wet. Use a 3 oz cup to form mixture and invert mixture onto serving plate. Serve with canolis and black bean sauce. Garnish with celery sprig or deep fried onion rings.

DESSERTS

HENRY MORGAN'S PRIDE

Bread pudding served atop a dark rum sauce. Page 49

A CHRISTMAS TIME

A chocolate fruit cake served atop amaretto sauce. Page 51

COCONUT MADNESS

A coconut cake laced with a sweet coconut sauce. Page 53

DREAM SO SWEET

A banana cake topped with sautéed bananas and mango puree flavoured with vanilla and cinnamon. Page 55

MIDDLE SOFT

Cornmeal pudding glazed with a creamy coconut sauce. Page 57

PIRATE'S BOUNTY

A light pastry filled with guava and served with a hard sauce. Page 59

HENRY MORGAN'S PRIDE

Bread Pudding Served Atop A Dark Rum Sauce

Rum Sauce

1 1/2 cups Appleton dark rum
3/4 cup brown sugar
1 tablespoon butter
1 teaspoon vanilla
1 tablespoon cornstarch

Ready!
In small saucepan over low flame, heat butter and add cornstarch. Add sugar, dark rum and vanilla. Let reduce for 2-3 minutes over a high flame. Pour over bread pudding.

Pudding

9 slices raisin bread
1 cup ripe bananas, sliced
6 tablespoons butter
3 eggs
2 1/4 cups coconut milk
1 1/4 cups whole milk
3 teaspoons vanilla
1 teaspoon cinnamon
1 teaspoon nutmeg
1 pinch salt
1 1/2 cups brown sugar
1/2 cup almonds, chopped
1 ripe banana, sliced
1/2 cup American apple, peeled, sliced

Ready!
Butter each slice of bread and tear into small pieces. In large mixing bowl, combine eggs, milk, butter, vanilla, cinnamon, nutmeg, salt and sugar. Mix in bread, almonds and banana. Pour mixture into a greased baking tin and bake at 325° degrees F for 25 minutes. Serve hot and top with rum sauce. Decorate with apple slice and mint.

A Christmas Time

A Chocolate Fruit Cake Served Atop Amaretto Sauce

Cake
1 box Betty Crocker German Chocolate cake mix
2 cups all-purpose flour
1/4 cup oil
1 teaspoon baking soda
3/4 cup amaretto
3 eggs
1 1/2 cups raisins
1 cup red wine
1 cup maraschino cherries, halved
1 teaspoon cinnamon
1 teaspoon nutmeg

Ready!
In blender, blend raisins and red wine. Set aside. In electric mixer combine eggs, oil, cake mix and baking soda. Slowly add amaretto and mix in well adding 2 cups flour. Fold in maraschino cherries and raisins and red wine mixture, and spices. Pour into greased baking tin and bake at 325° degrees F for 35 minutes. Decorate with whip cream and mint.

Amaretto Sauce
1 cup amaretto
1 teaspoon cinnamon
1/2 cup wine
1 teaspoon cornstarch

Combine cornstarch, wine and cinnamon in small bowl. In a small saucepan, heat amaretto over a low flame. Add wine mixture and let reduce for 3 minutes over a medium flame. Stir constantly. When mixture appears syrupy it is done.

COCONUT MADNESS

A Coconut Cake Laced With A Sweet Coconut Sauce

Cake

2 cups all-purpose flour
1 tablespoon baking powder
1 teaspoon salt
1 1/4 cups sugar
3 eggs
1 3/4 cups coconut milk
1 cup coconut, grated
1 teaspoon vanilla
1 teaspoon cinnamon
1 teaspoon nutmeg
1 cup butter

Ready!
In large bowl, sieve flour, salt, cinnamon, baking powder and nutmeg and set aside. In an electric mixer, cream together butter and sugar light and fluffy. On a low speed, add eggs 1 at a time with a 30-second interval. Add 1 cup of flour mixture then mix in slowly one cup of milk and vanilla. Add remaining flour and coconut flakes. Mix in remaining coconut milk and pour mixture into a greased baking tin. Bake at 325° degrees F for 30 minutes or until done. Decorate with coconut flakes and sugar glaze.

Sugar Glaze

1 cup dark sugar
2 teaspoons vanilla
1 cup coconut milk
1/2 teaspoon cinnamon

Ready!
In a saucepan, bring milk to a boil and add sugar. Add vanilla and cinnamon. Let mixture reduce for 6 minutes over high flame or until the mixture becomes syrupy. Top each serving of coconut cake with glaze.

DREAM SO SWEET

A Banana Cake Topped With Sauteed Bananas And Mango Puree Flavoured With Vanilla And Cinnamon

Cake

2 cups all-purpose flour
1 teaspoon salt
3/4 cup sugar, dark
3 eggs
1 teaspoon vanilla
1 teaspoon cinnamon
1 cup ripe bananas, pureed
1 cup mango, ripe, pureed
1 teaspoon banana flavoring
1/2 cup oil
1 cup coconut milk
1 tsp baking soda

Ready!
In a large bowl sift together flour, baking soda, spices and salt using a strainer or sieve. In an electric mixer, beat eggs and sugar until smooth and slowly add oil. Fold in flour mixture slowly adding milk as mixture gets dry. Fold in banana puree, banana flavorings and vanilla. Pour into greased baking tin and bake at 325° degrees F for 30 minutes or until done.

Topping

2 cups sliced bananas
1/4 cup dark sugar
2 tablespoons butter
1 teaspoon vanilla

Ready!
In a small saucepan, heat butter and sauté bananas for 1 minute adding vanilla and sugar. Remove from heat and serve over each slice of banana cake. Decorate with slices of mango.

MIDDLE SOFT

Cornmeal Pudding Glazed With Creamy Coconut Sauce

Pudding

2 1/2 cups yellow cornmeal
1/2 cup condensed milk, sweetened
2 cups evaporated milk
1/4 cup sugar, refined
1 teaspoon cinnamon
1 cup raisins
3 cups coconut milk
1/4 cup butter
2 tablespoons vanilla
1 tablespoon nutmeg
1 teaspoon salt

Ready!
In a medium pot, bring coconut milk, condensed milk and whole milk to a boil. Add cornmeal, sugar, vanilla, nutmeg, cinnamon, salt and butter. Use a whisk and stir constantly to prevent lumps. When mixture thickens, add raisins and remove from flame. Pour mixture into a greased baking tin and top with coconut topping.

Topping

1/2 cup whole milk
1/2 cup coconut milk
1/2 cup condensed milk
1 teaspoon cinnamon
1 teaspoon vanilla
1 teaspoon nutmeg

Ready!
In a small bowl, combine whole milk, coconut milk, condensed milk, cinnamon, vanilla and nutmeg. Slowly pour 1/4 cup of the topping over the pudding mixture and bake at 325 degrees F for 20 minutes, and top again with mixture. Continue baking for 35 minutes or until the pudding is golden brown and slightly firm. Serve in a small bowl and decorate with cherries and cinnamon sticks.

Tip:

This pudding is also great with Rum Sauce! (See HENRY MORGAN'S PRIDE recipe on page 49)

PIRATE'S BOUNTY

A Light Pastry Filled With Guava And Served With A Hard Sauce

Guava Duff

2 1/2 cups guava, tin, drained
1 tablespoon baking powder
1 cup sugar
1 1/2 cups butter
3 cups self-rising flour
1 teaspoon salt
1 teaspoon cinnamon
2 eggs, beaten

Ready!

In a small bowl, mince guava using a knife and set aside. In a large bowl sieve flour, baking powder, sugar, salt and cinnamon, and cut in butter using a pastry cutter. Flour mixture should look like breadcrumbs. Blend the mixture using beaten eggs. Form the mixture into a ball and roll out into a rectangle. Dust with flour and spread guava mixture over the dough leaving a 1 inch margin around the dough. Roll dough into a log and carefully loosely wrap the dough in aluminum foil leaving enough space for the dough to rise while cooking. Carefully seal the dough again with the aluminum foil leaving enough space for the dough to rise. Boil the foil package in a large pot of boiling water for 30 minutes. Carefully remove from the water without perforating the foil. Remove foil and cut 1 inch slices. Serve with a hard sauce and decorate with mint.

Hard Sauce

2 cups icing sugar
1 cup butter
1/2 cup guava, tin, drained

Ready!

In electric mixer cream icing sugar, butter and guava until smooth. Let mixture cool for 10 minutes. Place 2-4 slices of guava duff on an oven-proof serving plate and top with 1 spoon of hard sauce and bake at 320 degrees F for 5 minutes. Serve hot.

Tip:

Guava Duff can also be baked in foil package. Be sure to place a pan of water on the lowest shelf and bake foil package on a tray over the water. When using this method bake at 325° degrees F for 40 minutes.

METRIC CONVERSION TABLE

To Change	To	Multiply by
Oz.	G	28
Lbs.	Kg	.45
Tsp.	Ml	5
Tbsp.	Ml	15
Fl. Oz.	Ml	30
Cups	L	.24
Degrees F	Degrees C	5/9 after subtracting 32

Glossary

Oz - Ounce
Lbs - Pounds
Tsp. - Teaspoon
Tbsp - Tablespoon
Fl. Oz - Fluid Ounce

What does this mean?

Callaloo?

This is a green leafy vegetable very much like spinach and you can substitute callaloo with spinach. It's a traditional Jamaican favorite for breakfast, lunch or dinner. I simply adore callaloo in soups!

Yam?

Pretty much like potatoes but yams have a firmer texture. Yellow, white and purple yams are widely used in Jamaica, Puerto Rico and the Dominican Republic.

Pimento?

This is a secret ingredient to great recipes! The Pimento comes from the pimento berry and is slightly spicy with a sweet aroma. Just look for Jamaican pimento in the supermarket, it's a great spice to have in your kitchen!

INDEX